Fantasy, Fact and Fun

but

Mostly Fantasy

BY

Sam MacEachan

Drawings and Design by Ann Macmillan

CONTENTS

Bliss

No wealth do I require,
I all ambition shun,
I have but one desire—
A hammock in the sun.

There I would lie at ease
And spend the idle hours
In list'ning to the bees
Amidst the idle flowers.

I'd watch the branches sway
Across the azure sky,
And see the squirrels play
As idle clouds swam by.

In lethargy I'd sink,
But though I'd idle seem,
I've idle thoughts to think
And idle dreams to dream.

So that I do not tire,
With so much to be done,
I really must acquire
A hammock in the sun.

....

Peace

Let others prate if babbling brooks;
Of sylvan scenes and such,
For winding ways and shady nooks
Don't charm me very much.

Nor does the green and gentle hill,
Nor do the distant mountains,
Where rills and rivers run to fill
The waterfalls and fountains.

Some quietly speak of the long peace
Which we shall all inherit,.
When toils and cares and troubles cease
And Man becomes a Spirit.

There is another peace and rest
Which isn't so alarming.
I find it on my lover's breast
And's certainly more charming.

But 'Peace' , to me, is best defined
In words of small amount –
'A healthy body; healthy mind
And healthy bank account.'
....

To a Seedling

Brave seedling, tiny and courageous weed
Pale offspring of the thistle, hither brought
By wayward winds, alas! thy parents' seed
Must come to naught.

Thou wert intended from thy birth to grace
The by-ways and the lanes, but thou hast found
No rich sustaining earth, or grassy place,
But barren ground.

Unkind the fate that set thee here to strive
Alone, in this unsympathetic soil,
Where thou, undaunted, only can survive
With endless toil.

If only in some garden thou hadst grown;
In deep-delved earth; in flow'ring border wide,
Thy crowned purple blooms thou couldst have shown
With modest pride.

But thou wilt not, poor seedling, ever flow'r,
Yet thou must reach forever for the sky
And struggle upwards all thy little hour
-- And so must I.

....

Resurrection

When we are dead it matters not
That those we love are living yet,
For they are by the dead forgot
And soon the living, too, forget.

Perhaps <u>your</u> clay, anourishing
The earth that you have left behind,
Will feed the flow'rs there flourishing
And bring your mem'ry back to mind.

But this, <u>my</u> flesh, will turn to dust
And lie upon some country lane,
And then a wind will come, I trust,
To lift me swiftly up again.

No gentle zephyr! but a breeze
Of boist'rous moods and gusty mirth,
That whips the grass, assails the trees,
And we shall gaily roam the Earth.

Then I shall gaze from Heav'n a while,
To where the Earth's by dust beset,
And I shall smile a secret smile
To see that I am living yet!

....

Pessimism

Oh! come with me and let us go
To some far place beyond the sun,
Where perfect peace the people know
And ev'ryone loves ev'ryone;
Where there's no hate, or greed, or sin;
Where base ambition is unknown;
Where petty pride can't enter in;
From where the lust for pow'r has flown.

No church, or mosque, or dome will stand,
As they so long on Earth have done,
For, in the far-off happy land,
There'll be one faith for ev'ryone.
There'll be no need for songs of praise;
No need for prayer, or psalm, or hymn,
For, seeing God's proud smiling face,
We'll wave a friendly hand to Him.

Oh! hurry, Love, and let us soar
Through outer-space to ev'rywhere,
And there we'll range for ever-more,
To seek a world that is not there.
....

To Grandson Eric

Play with thy teddy bear and toys
As long's thou canst, the years
Too soon will pass and leave behind
Their legacies of tears.

Too soon wilt thou forget the woes
That grieve and vex thee now,
Too soon will sterner trials leave
Their imprint on thy brow.

Cling to thy mother's apron strings
Till thou art older grown,
Yet learn thou wilt, as learn thou must,
That thou must stand alone.

Yea, thou must stand alone and face
Whatever may befall,
Yet will a stout and manly heart
Endure or conquer all.

If thou canst but endure the fray,
Though 'tis by others won,
Then is the final triumph thine,
And thine alone, my son.

....

Only Four

My sister is more big than me
By half a head or more,
For she is nearly six, you see,
And I am only four.

We play together all day long,
Our play I do enjoy,
But she gets rough because she's strong
And I'm a little boy.

She teases me a lot, you know,
And pulls me on the floor,
And takes my toys away although
She knows I'm only four.

And, sometimes, when she pushes me,
I cry a bit, but then
I am only four, you see.
Just wait till I am ten!

....

The Seventh Day

It really isn't true to say,
—No matter what my mum says—
That, having worked till Saturday,
God said "I'll not work Sundays."

Because He said "Good gracious Me!
I've made the sun and showers,
But they no earthly good will be
Unless I make some flowers."

"I'll have to make them right away;
The children will expect them
And what would little children say
If I were to neglect them?"

I'll have to get up with the dawn
And make them all on one day."
And so, with love, He made them on
The next day – which was SUNDAY.

....

Affections

I love to see a calm blue sky
Above a calm blue sea,
I love the glens and mountains high;
The moorlands wild and free;
The rolling hills and valleys there,
I love, well —————— nearly ev'rywhere.

I love to see the birth of Spring;
New leaves upon the trees;
The crocus brightly flourishing;
To feel a warmer breeze.
I love to hear a blackbird sing,
I love, well ——————- nearly ev'rything.

I love to see a baby smile;
To see young children play.
I love to talk with friends a while
To pass the time of day,
But then, when all is said and done,
I love, well ——————- nearly ev'ryone.

....

My Love

My Love is a lady of two years and twenty,
Sweet as a morning in May and as fair,
With graces abounding and virtues aplenty;
Stars in her eyes and the sun in her hair.

My Love is a lady, so graceful and slender,
Blest with the beauties denied to the rose,
The nightingales hearing her voice, sweet and tender,
Falter and then bring their songs to a close.

The songs of the birds and the beauties of flowers,
These are distractions I treat with disdain.
I seek but to pass in oblivion the hours
Till I shall see my beloved again.

Lady, my lady, despair lies upon me,
Lest I may ne'er know your presence again,
Yet shall I constantly keep close before me,
Mem'ries that always shall with me remain.

....

An Early Love

My love was a lady whose years were uncounted,
Sour as a plum early plucked from the tree,
Her language was filthy, her virtues discounted
By Tom, Dick, and Harry and Sandy and me.

Her figure was plump, for her curves they went out and
At various places swept lusciously in.
She owned to a liking for Guiness's stout and
She pampered an o'erpow'ring passion for gin.

And this was the lady who caused all the bother
To my young heart when I fondly adored!
Thank heavens that I took a look at her mother;
Saw she I loved would be later abhorred.

Oh, blest be the year and the day and the hour
That stopped for all time her dire need of my name,
For while the dew glistened I savoured the flower,
Till she met another and married the same.

....

The Elderly Admirer

I gave to my lady a message of greeting,
Revealing the love which had sprung from my heart,
And begging that she would agree to a meeting
And that from my side she would never depart.

Her smile is so gentle and sweetly disarming,
Bewitching and lovely the light in her eyes,
Her figure is lithesome and gracefully charming,
Sne satisfied all of my dreams and desires.

My thoughts were devoted alone to my dearie,
All day and all night –the full twentyfour hours–
I sailed through life happily, hopeful and cheery,
And dreamed of the bliss which would surely be ours.

But Time has, alas! put an end to such notions
–Some things which are gone cannot ever return–
So now I must stifle all tender emotions
And wander alone on the banks of the Earn.

But, Lyn, it may be that some centuries later
We'll meet once again and discover, at last,
That Time is more kindly than once we had thought her
And we'll know the bliss which we missed in the past.

Remorse

She came across the fields to me
On dancing feet; with laughing eyes.
The sight of her enchanted me.
Naught did I know nor yet surmise
Of what the future held for us.
Weep for us.

A nosegay blossomed on her breast,
Her cheeks were flushed with happiness.
Sweet innocence with beauty dressed,
I ne'er had seen such loveliness.
She held her red lips up to me.
Weep for me.

I took her beauty and I crushed
Her nosegay as I slaked my lust,
Then saw the tears that downwards gushed
And all my pleasure was as dust.
I could not bear to look at her.
Weep for her.

....

Fulfilment

Some day I'll find you waiting all alone
Upon some distant undiscovered strand,
While, from a sea lit by a moon unknown,
The placid wavelets creep o'er silver sand,
And there will be, I think, a scented breeze;
The perfume of a hundred thousand flowers;
The fragrance of ten thousand forest trees
And dreams of youth and happy golden hours.
Then eagerly along the beech I'll race
And you will see me come with glad surprise.
Until, united in a fierce embrace,
We drown together in each other's eyes,
But I shall know that now Time's race is run
And, at the last, I've lost all I have won.

....

What is Love?

Two young people, all their being
Swearing love and constancy,
Each one in the other seeing
Things no other eye can see.
Maybe this is love.

Newly-weds, forever petting,
Window-shopping, looking at
Cots and prams and ever fretting
At the cost of this and that.
Well – this *might* be love.

See that couple over yonder,
Buxom wife and city gent?
Does one ever pause to ponder
How the other's day is spent?
Their relationship's about it,
As they raise their growing brood,
Something of the force of habit,
Friendship mixed with frequent feud.
But there *could* be love.

There's a couple, children married,
Happy now to take it slow,
Free of work, by care unharried,
As the bonds between them grow.
This *could well* be love.

Two old friends, their ending sharing,
Silent, still, their journey done,
Each, while waiting, only caring,
Caring for the other one.
This *indeed* is love.

....

Tae a Deid Rat

Pair beastie, deid and lyin' there
Amang the fallen rubble,
There's naethin' in my garden here
That could be worth yir trouble.

The grun' is bare, the frost in keen
An' snell the wind that's blawin',
An' in the sky it can be seen
That soon it will be snawin'.

But ye cam in an' met the fate
That struck ye unobservit.
Tae tell the truth ye were na blate
An' weel ye did deserve it.

Yir no a very cheery sicht!
In faith, ye are na bonny.
Ye've gi'en folks mony an unco fricht
An' me as much as ony.

Although ye are a cratur wha
Is feared by man an' woman,
There's plenty ither vermin tae
An' some o' them are human.

But though ye are a rat indeed,
An' wi' a stane's been skelpit,
Yet ye're a rat as Fate decreed
An' sae ye canna help it.

....

The Coup de Grace

The Raging fires within the restless Earth,
And pressures vast, time after time have torn
Deep chasms in the surface, given birth
To soaring mountain ranges that have born
The rancour of relentless wind and rain;
Of bitter frost and grinding ice and snow
That have, in time, reduced them grain by grain
And brought their proud and lofty summits low.
So I, a man once full of manly pride,
Have by the icy word; the frosty frown,
Been worn away, submissively to bide,
And all my male conceit has crumbled down.
But yet, the wifely wile I mostly fear
Is still the quiv'ring lip; the trembling tear.

....

For a Stranger

They came along the pavement wet,
They are–in–arm like lovers were,
And they were strangers to me yet
My heart at once went out to her.

And, as they passed, she smiled to me,
And very briefly met my eyes,
Then turned away, lest I should see
Her puzzled look and faint surmise.

I knew that we had never met,
But I was equally surprised.
We did not know each other yet
Each other we'd half-recognised.

14

What then the link? What then the bond?
What the affinity that could
Draw us together to respond
To something we'd not understood?

Perhaps when Earth was fresh and young,
And clean the garments that it wore,
I'd lived with her and laughed and sung
Of love on that far distant shore

Where Zeus upon Olympus dwelt
With all his careless brood, and in
Their temples graceful people knelt
And none had yet invented sin.

Could it have been that we had met,
But did another life pursue?
Had she, perhaps, been Juliet
And I a son to Montague?

I watched them go. The wind and rain
Revealed her grace; her figure trim.
I saw her twice look back again
And yearned for her, and envied him.

I turned and lit a cigarette,
When from my sight they both had gone.
I braved the dusk, so cold and wet,
And then I sadly plodded on.

To the Wedding Guests
23rd June, 1990

Our thanks for being midst the throng
Of our dear friends, to see us wed.
Right joyously we start along
The unknown road which lies ahead.

The road's unknown, but yet we know
That all along it we shall find
It leads, however far we go,
To sweet content and peace of mind.

And when we're nearing journey's end,
And Bruce is bald and Christa's grey,
We'll still remember ev'ry friend
Who came to share this happy day.

Cherry

My love has asked me for a rhyme
Upon a subject dreary,
For which I've neither wit nor time
And my poor Muse is weary.
She'll neither sing a song that's sad
Nor yet a song that's merry,
Nor will she sing a gay *ballade*,
She'll only sing of Cherry.

Lines Written in Saint Michael's Kirkyard, Crieff.

Here lie the bones of one unknown,
Unknown his name and year of birth,
His tombstone lies wrecked, overthrown,
Face-down upon the sacred earth.

Here, in this quiet hallowed ground,
They laid him down within his lair,
And then with wreaths the grave they crowned,
And tearfully they left him there.

They left him there in peace to sleep
Among the friends who round him lay,
Until the time for him to keep
His tryst with God on Judgement Day.

In summer-time the hawthorn tree
The warm and gentle air perfumed,
And o'er the kirkyard ev'rywhere
The buttercups and daisies bloomed.

But now it is a place forlorn,
Where desolation reigns instead,
With none to grieve; with none to mourn,
Or to revere the ancient dead.

Alas! the dead have no redress;
None to protect their sad domain
From time and impious hands unless
Saint Michael aids them once again.

....

On a Theme by Christopher Marlowe

The Proposition.

From this dull city let us fly
To where the air is sweet,
Where hov'ring song-birds grace the sky
And grass is neath our feet.

There let us seek some shady dell
Beneath the beeches' boughs
And, while we free and tranquil dwell,
Redeem our loving vows.

The hyacinth and violet
Shall decorate your bow'r,
And in content we shall forget
To mark the passing hour.

The blackbird and the lark will sing
Their morning songs of praise.
Their liquid notes will surely bring
Enchantment to our days.

And ev'ry morn I'll bring to you
The fruits of vale and hill,
And bathing in the morning dew
Will make you lovelier still.

Before the trees their blossoms shed,
These pleasures yours will be.
Of fern and moss shall be our bed
If you will live with me.

The Reply.

I would not in the country dwell.
I like not sylvan bowers.
I do not want a shady dell
Though carpeted with flowers.

With birdsong in the early morn
I firmly disagree,
And bathing in the dew – *at dawn!*
Does not appeal to me.

My taste runs more to simple things
More practical than flowers,
Like heating and a w.c.
And baths and bath-room showers.

And carpets fitted wall to wall,
A kitchen clean and bright,
A telephone inside the hall,
A lounge both large and light.

A shopping centre, most of all,
Must be near our menage
And, so I'll reach a bingo hall,
A car in our garage.

A well-sprung mattress on the bed
To me, I think, is due,
But first of all, my friend, we'll wed
Before I live with you.

The Secret Place
(A True Story)

There is was! A gleaming cluster
In a clearing in the wood,
Where it gained an added lustre
From a sunbeam's golden flood.

Primroses! each open petal
Halo–ed by a sunny ray,
Luminous as precious metal,
Fresh and clean as was the day.

Green the grass around them growing,
They like shining jewels shone,
As might yellow diamonds glowing
On the baize they lie upon.

Tenderly, a sky unclouded
Hovered o'er the silent ring
Of the trees that closely crowded,
Verdant with the leaves of Spring.

Somehow feeling I intruded,
I could sense an atmosphere
Strangely holy. Scent exuded
Incense–like from blossoms there.

Did the trees come even closer,
Reverently worshipping?
Was that secret small enclosure
Altar of Spring's burgeoning?

Had it once been consecrated
To the rites of pagan Pan,
Or to Flora dedicated
– Where her floral fiat ran?

Or was this a tiny remnant
Of a world that few did see,
Where–in Eve, the unrepentant,
Plucked the apple from the tree?

This I know not, but I listened,
Not a sound or movement made,
While the cluster glowed and glistened
In that secret sinless glade.

Where no man had penetrated,
I lay quietly concealed,
And I tensely watched and waited
For what then might be revealed.

But the sunbeam faded fleetly,
And the upper branches sighed,
As the magic went completely,
When, alas! the sunbeam died.

Nonetheless I then departed
Down a path the trees between,
Elevated, happy–hearted,
More than I had ever been.

Now, when absently I ponder
On the mystery of love,
Elfin–like my fancies wander
To that far enchanted grove.

....

The House

Last night, beside a lonely road,
I saw a house, near tumbled down,
But at the door a lantern glowed
And light from broken windows showed
Through curtains torn and brown.

And music, frolicsome and free,
Assailed the brooding list'ning night,
And with that sound of revelry
Came peals of laughter, merrily,
And cries of deep delight.

To my surprise, I heard the sound
Of hoof–beats and of wheels approach,
As though, in haste, through dark profound,
To that secluded house was bound
A swiftly–moving coach.

And, as the noise of harness grew,
And as the the drumming hoof–beats neared,
A growing chilly dread I knew,
For, when they should have come in view,
No horse or coach appeared.

The coach pulled up, as I supposed,
I heard no hail or answ'ring shout:
The front door opened; ere it closed
No one the light within disclosed,
No one went in or out.

Then piercingly a woman screamed,
Her cry of terror rent the gloom,
The music stopped, no lantern gleamed,
No light from broken windows streamed:
The house was like a tomb.

A cock crew twice to greet the day,
The early-morning air grew chill
And, from that house of slow decay,
I heard the horses speed away
Then all was hushed and still.

The roofless house stood all alone,
No smoke from any chimney strayed,
But with it's eyeless face of stone
To me, somehow, it seemed to own
That it was sore afraid.

....

In Haste

This is no mere fleeting greeting
Or a friendly note, or such,
But a declaration, sweeting,
That I love you very much.

All day long I try to capture
Visions of your lovely face
And, all night, I lie in rapture
Dreaming of your poise and grace.

Though with ardour I am burning
And deep passions in me lurk,
Soon the boss will be returning
So I must get back to work.

....

Caprice

Daisy, daisy, daisy sweet,
Tell me, if you can,
When I yet again shall meet
My young gentleman.

Daisy, daisy, tell me, do
Tell me, if you will,
Is my lover fond and true?
Does he love me still?

Daisy, daisy, daisy, pray,
If you can then tell
What your pretty petals say.
Does he love me well?

He loves me. He love me not.
Daisy, is this so?
Have I been by him forgot?
How can petals know?

Ah! he loves me yet again!
Oh! he loves me never!
Ah! he loves me and 'tis plain
He will love me ever.

Daisy petals, blowing free,
Sudden is my whim.
Tell the gentleman for me
That I don't love him.

24

To a Hoped-For Grandson.

What keeps you boy? You're very late!
Your grandad's been in such a state
At having all this time to wait,
But, though you're late-come,
You can be sure, at any rate,
You'll be most welcome.

It's like enough while you're a lad
He'll take you out and he'll be glad
To tell you of the times he's had,
And he'll be wishin',
Unless it's by your mum forbad,
To take you fishin'.

He's also sure that you and he,
—Your daddy too, of course— will be,
When you're grown up, like cronies three,
(It's wishful thinkin')
And ever ready on a spree
To go off drinkin'.

He says he knows you'll join the crew
Of his dream yacht and sail out to
Some tropic isle out in the blue,
Perhaps to Haiti.
When you are seventeen, mark you,
He'll be near eighty.

But lad, your grandad always seems
To be engrossed in hapless schemes
And oft his eye with fancy gleams.
It may be you can
Resist the lure and charm of dreams.
I'm damned if he can.

....

For My Scots/Norwegian Grandson – Sam Andreas

A thousand years have gone, and more
Since Viking raiders reached the shore
Of Scotland's western highlands.
They came with axes, spears and swords
And, for a while, were overlords
Of Hebridean islands.

To heathen gods they prayed and swore
By mighty Odin and by Thor,
The gods of war and thunder.
Their courage and their swords prevailed
When into distant seas they sailed,
In search of land and plunder.

They came in summer, when the sea
From storm was relatively free
And kindlier it's motion.
Their ships, with high up-curving prows,
They rowed and sailed until their bows
Had cleaved th'Atlantic ocean.

Right fearsomely they were arrayed.
Of iron swords and spears were made:
Their shields were iron studded
And, once ashore, they silent crept
Then on their victims swiftly leapt,
And soon their swords were blooded.

They sailed the seas from Stornoway
And took whatever came their way,
And slaughtered without pity.
They were the terror of the seas,
These pirates of the Hebrides,
From Unst to Dublin City.

They roamed the islands far and wide,
Despoiling all the countryside
And burning farm and village
Until, at last, there came the day
These summer-sailors sailed away,
When tired of rape and pillage.

But in the Spring they fast returned,
But they no longer robbed and burned
Or with the people feuded.
This time they came to colonise
Where once they sought to terrorise
And leave the land denuded.

And now, my grandson, you've contrived
To meet me here and have arrived
Direct from Heaven's portal,
So when my time is come I know
I'll gladly to Valhalla go,
Contented and immortal.

....

Clan Ranald

A Meditation at the Gravesides of Culloden.

Afar, the golden eagle lonely glides
O'er what was once the home of mountaineers.
Now, scattered sheep graze on the mountainsides
'bove which Ben Resipol o'erlooks his peers.
A range of bare and serried mountains guards
The long and silv'ry finger of Loch Shiel
That straightly, from th'Atlantic, points towards
The greener gentler lands of famed Lochiel.
There, once, did men of ancient Celtic blood
Hold sway among their mountain fastnesses,
And that is where they valiantly withstood
The few who dared assail their fortresses.
They also were of Donald's; Ranald's blood,
Innured to strife and war, they e'er defied
The outside hostile world. They only had
Their weapons, cattle, kinship and their pride.
Obedience only to one man they gave
And to that man alone they gave acclaim;
In peace a counsellor and in battle brave,
Their chief and Representer of The Name.
At his command they sallied forth to war,
As once they went with Bruce to stand and fight,
To gain, at Bannockburn, for evermore,
The privilege of fighting on the right.
"My Hope is Constant in Thee", cried the king.
That hope, that faith, they never did betray,
For to the Stewart cause they e'er did cling;
Their blood like water flowed in each affray.
So Edward learned to fear the highland host,
—Brief the encounter, briefer his farewell!—
And many were the battles Argyll lost,
And many were the Campbell men who fell,
As when, for gain, they in rebellion rose
And northwards marched to Inverlochy's shore,
But fast returned before the great Montrose;

Before Clan Ranald's men. MacCailein Mor,
To later gain a shameful victory,
Lived on and Stewart kings still briefly wore
Th'uneasy crown, but this proud history
Alas! was ended on Culloden Moor.

My heart with anguish fills when I recall
The story of that day with horror filled.
I almost *see* th'exhausted valiant fall
And hear the cries as wounded men are killed.
Here Bloody William earned inglorious fame
–Not only from his slaughtered enemy–
And added to the Hanoverian name
A further crown of damned infamy.
Clan Ranald's dead were buried where they were,
The race's virtues never more displayed,
And those who once cried out "Gainsay Who Dare",
For ever after were to be gainsaid.

The golden eagle glides o'er his demesne,
A lifeless landscape giv'n to sheep and trees,
Indiff'rent mountains, ageless and serene,
Hear but the winter's wind; the summer's breeze.
Not now is heard the cattle's bellowing,
The children's laughter rises up no more
And ne'er the sound of pibrochs echoing
Clan Ranald's call to foray or to war.

Stay, brother, stay and give a timely thought.
These men, who came from distant homes to die,
For James and 'gainst the hated Union fought,
Spare, then, a tear and sympathetic sigh.
No glory did the victor garner here,
The laurel slipped from off his bloody brow,
Compassion fell beneath the feet of Fear,
Where only Grief and Pity linger now.

....

The Ruined Cot

Whose were the hands which touched this stone and raised
These cottage walls, now tumbled down, alas!
While on these slopes his scattered cattle grazed
Upon the luscious early–summer grass?

With weary steps and almost endless toil
He must have searched for stones upon the hill;
With bloody hands have torn them from the soil
And ever found that more were needed still.

Perhaps he laboured joyfully and oft,
With willing heart, upon this mountainside,
That he might soon bring home to this same croft
Some simple lass – his newly–wedded bride.

It may have been that, ere his task was done;
Before his hearth had felt the kiss of fire,
He heard the call to aid his monarch's son
Regain the throne for his long–exiled sire

And, following the long exhausting road
That led, at last, to far Culloden Muir,
He may have there put down the earthly load
His wounded body could no more endure.

But let us hope he lived in peace to see
His cattle prosper on the grassy slopes,
And happy children cluster round his knee
To crown, with artless love, his dearest hopes.

Whoe'er he was, whate'er his fate, amid
His native bens and hills, he left us here
No sculptured sphinx or princely pyramid,
But just the humble walls he held so dear.

The Fairies' Curse

I wish I knew if it is true
That Little People, lying
All snug and sound beneath the ground,
Can hear a baby crying.

It may be they, as some folk say,
When babies they discover,
Will often thieve, as some believe,
The baby from it's mother.

And crofters who don't pay their due
Of cream and milk to fairies,
Will often find that left behind
Are spells upon their dairies.

It well may be that they will see
The milk which they are churning,
Within the hour all wersh and sour
Has all the time been turning.

And, what is worse, the spiteful curse
The fairies have inflicted,
May in the fields reduce the yields
And leave the beasts afflicted.

It may be so. I only know
To ward off spells enchanted,
A rowan tree, as all agree,
Must near at hand be planted.

No tree I'd plant! If fairies scant
Of milk and cream, at leisure
Will leave a pail of heather ale,
I'll give them milk with pleasure.

....

The Diamond Tree

How I long for a glimpse of my mountains again,
With their craggy heads covered with snow,
While the great golden eagle glides over the glen
And the onrushing river below.

When the air, still and clear from the winter's embrace,
Is aglow from the kiss of the sun,
On the frost—covered gorse it is easy to trace
All the webs which the spiders have spun.

And I think of the beauty revealed to me,
On a day when the morning was young,
When I saw on the tip of each leaf of a tree,
That a glittering diamond was hung.

On that breath—taking vision i often reflect,
And the mem'ry can never be lost
Of that exquisite birch with it's diamonds, bedecked
And adorned by the ice and the frost.

The enchantments of nature are open to me,
They my heart and my fancy beguile,
And the loveliest visions I constantly see
Of my dear distant home in Argyll.

....

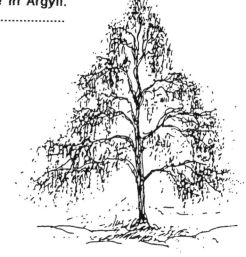

Foyers

Here I work from eight till six
And a mass of concrete mix.
In it now thou hast been cast
And shall soon be fixed fast,
Never more to see the sun
For thy careless days are done.

Thus I've saved thee from the bane
Of eroding wind and rain,
So that thou shalt be preserved
And for useful life reserved,
Serving man as best's ye may,
Serving him for many a day.

When ten thousand years are gone,
(After I have journeyed on)
Then by cataclysm vast
Thou *mayst* see the light at last.
Shouldst again the sun thou see,
Little pebble, think of me.

....

Yearnings

All the birds and the flowers say springtime is here,
The beat of my heart says it too,
And the lambs and the blossoms begin to appear,
Fresh life to the land comes anew,
And the song of the thrush on the apple-trees bough,
And the first flush of daffodils, tell me that now
Is the season for loving and mating, somehow
I know that my true-love is near.

In the fullness of summer we'll carelessly lie
The whole of each long sunny day,
And we'll see the white clouds floating lazily by,
And drink in the scent of the hay.
I can see it all now and although you may deem
It the airiest fancy, and such it may seem,
Yet I know it is something much more than a dream,
And more than a wish or a sigh.

....

The Lost Love

Still, sometimes even now, the thought of you
Seeps softly and unbidden to my heart,
And overflows, and fills up ev'ry part
Of this vast void within me. Then a new
And gently-spreading warmth engulfs me quite
And bathes my soul a little space, and then
Just as it came, it slowly fades again,
As fades the dawn that falsely ends the night.
'tis then that hell's black squadrons swiftly surge
From out the gloomy caverns of my mind:
In grim and unrelenting waves they charge
And I'm o'erwhelmed anew. Their sharp spears find
Each chink; each breach; each quiv'ring wound and then
They disappear, and I'm alone again.

....

The Death of Hope

Lovely Hope has gone away,
Fair she was and kind,
Sombre Sorrow's come to stay,
Troubled is my mind.

Whither, whither shall I seek?
Whither does she dwell?
Midst a city's noise and reek
Or in quiet dell?

Does she live with Ignorance?
Does she live with Truth?
Does she live with Innocence?
Does she live with Love?

Does she dwell with Luxury
Or in dwelling crude?
Does she live with Penury
Or with Solitude?

****

Quiet, friend, and be at ease.
Trouble not your breath.
Hope resides with none of these.
Hope resides with Death.

....

The Sea

My God! Just feel it's mindless strength; it's force;
It's pow'r implacable; it's monst'rous might;
It's overwhelming magnitude! Yet our frail bark
Rests like a child upon the bosom of Leviathan.
Just now it sleeps, but how uneasily,
For, like a glutted tiger in Bengal
That crouches with it's eyes
Half-open and it's claws but barely sheathed,
It rests in slumb'rous silence, but prepared
To spring up in an instant and attack
With savagery irresistible
And bared and frightful fangs, to tear and rend;
To batter, crush and to annihilate,
And we, who sail upon it's surface, float
Halfway between the sky and that dark land
That lies immeasurable depths below,
A dreadful world of shapes grotesque and gloom
So deep that it out-blackens black and hides
Th'encrusted bones of ships and men long dead.

Eighty

Behold my calm unfurrowed brow!
I'm free of toils and troubles, matey.
No woes or cares beset me now.
It's really lovely .... being eighty.

For riches I don't care a jot,
And now I think it's really funny
That once I even had to work
To lay my hands on any money!

Though now I miss the fond caress
That very often waited for me,
I'm fairly certain, nontheless,
That many ladies still adore me.

And this is rather nice, you know,
And if of this I wasn't certain,
I think I'd say "farewell" and go
And then pull down the final curtain.

....

Reverie

When memories return to me,
With all their joy and pain,
Then, like a child, I long to see
That dream-like world again,

Where days were long and full of sun,
And rain was never shed
And, when each golden day was done,
Our simple pray'rs were said.

Our childish words, pure and naive,
Were offered up to heaven
For God, we knew, would never grieve
A little lad of seven.

Ah! simple faith! unthinking trust!
God sees the sparrows fall,
But with what careless gaze He must
Observe them, one and all.

The time at school, the hours at play;
They altogether seem
Combined in some far yesterday
Or blended in a dream.

For innocence and artless joy
Those halcyon days were made,
When bliss was, to a little boy,
A bucket and a spade.

For fragile scuttling crabs amid
The tangled weed he pried,
Where in the rock-girt pools they hid,
Abandoned by the tide.

And in his painted bucket he
Would carry off his prize,
No doubt to die, but first to be
Admired by loving eyes.

Those loving eyes which quickly found
Whatever was amiss,
And saw that ev'ry graze was bound
Or mended with a kiss.

And father, somewhat more aloof,
—No kinder man was born—
My 'minister some small reproof,
Or else of danger warn.

The dullards, knaves and misers burn
To win the wealth they crave
And then, too late, they sadly learn
'tis naught beyond the grave,

And yet, that small and guileless boy,
Who knew not money's worth,
Could for a penny-piece enjoy
The treasures of the Earth.

A quiet mind is better far
Than pyramids of gold.
For those who Baal's disciples are
No passing-bell is tolled,

And he who so misled has been
Must count it as a loss
That he has not a mind serene,
  – That all he has is dross.

(over)

Alas! that five and fifty years
Have melted like the snow,
But in my mem'ry still appears
This dream of long ago,

And, as I view my prospects drear,
My vision blurs and I
Remember with a gentle tear;
With heart–ache and a sigh.

....

Sonnet

No man to any other man denies
His just and primal right to fall in love,
Nor yet to laud his dear one to the skies
And her all other charmers place above,
So I, enslaved by love–drugged senses,
Reel with burning passion many may deplore,
And unashamed infatuation feel
For her whose very perfume I adore.
Her charms are sprung from earth yet bloom like fire,
And health and wealth for her I throw away,
So uncontrollable is my desire
I consummate it twenty times a day
And then, with limbs relaxed and mind serene,
I venerate my mistress.......Nicotine.

....

NB. We have since parted.

40

Wisdom

Young Khalid worships in a mosque
Each Saturday and Sunday,
And Rachael in a synagogue,
Though she just goes on one day.

Now Kaysha, on the other hand,
—a Hindoo born and bred—
Does not attend a temple, but
Is taught at home instead.

Teresa is an Irish lass,
—She is quite young and pretty—
Who regularly goes to mass
With mum in Dublin City.

Johanna is a Protestant
Who goes to Sunday–school,
Where she is taught that Ulster can't
Submit to Popish rule.

To me it seems extremely odd
That people don't agree
To have, together, just one God
Instead of two or three.

They all say they have 'seen the light',
—They've stated this for long—
They cannot all, or course, be right,
Perhaps they all are wrong.

For though they say they know they know,
They do not know at all.
Because I know I do not know,
I'm wiser than them all.

The Sinner

Augustus Peter William Lee
Was quite a little lad,
When friends and neighbours found that he
Was very, very bad.

He loved to tease the little girls,
He loved to hear them squeal
When wickedly he pulled their curls,
A thing he did with zeal,

And ev'ry pup, and kitten too,
Would beat a sharp retreat
Whene'er they saw come into view
Augustus William Pete.

And when, like other little boys,
To school he had to go.
He'd scream and make a dreadful noise.
Quite often he said "No!"

When he was washed he'd be in tears
And make a fearful fuss,
Till papa had to box the ears
Of Peter William Gus.

By now he was so steeped in sin,
—I say it with regret—
That on one lovely summer's day
He smoked a cigarette!

He smoked it all, puff after puff,
And was extremely ill,
But he was made of rugged stuff,
Was Gussie Peter Bill.

Rejoicing in a life of crime,
He soon was smoking lots,
His face was rather pale, perhaps,
And rather full of spots.

It seems as though, I'm glad to say,
He's none the worse for it
And, even to the present day,
He looks quite well and fit.

And yet....and yet....it seems to me
He has a nasty cough.
I greatly fear that we may see
It carry Gussie off.

But he's grown up and has three sons
Who all look like their dad,
And we can only hope and pray
They won't be quite as bad.

....

The Happy Vagabond

I'm happy today, on this day in spring,
I'm happy because I've a song to sing,
Not a lass to plague, but a mossy bed
And a gentle breeze sighing overhead.

I'm happy·today, on this day in June,
I'm happy because all the afternoon
I shall laze away –for the sun is hot–
With a few more pints for the thirst I've got.

I'm happy today, though the autumn's chill,
I'm happy because I shall eat my fill,
I've a hunger got from the bracing air
And a pheasant too, and a nice fat hare.

I'm happy today, though the winter's here,
I'm happy because at this time of year
All the land is hushed, for it's gone to sleep,
And there's nothing moving, but grazing sheep.

I'm happy today and I go my way
With few to trouble or say me 'Nay',
For the road is open; the road is free,
And the world belongs to the likes of me.

The Blackbird

As I sat on the garden seat
-it was just yesterday-
A blackbird came and settled down
About twelve feet away.

The blackbird sat upon the ground
And not a feather stirred.
It neither moved or made a sound.
I uttered not a word.

'twas with delight and pleasure fond
I gazed, and I could see
There was a close and special bond
Between the bird and me.

My fathers had it's fathers known
When life on Earth was young.
Our bodies were of flesh and bone
And they from Earth had sprung.

Yet what I cannot understand
Is why to Earth we're driv'n,
When we would have been happier and
Much better off in Heaven,

For here we have to work and stay,
And here we live and die,
But why this is I cannot say
And none can tell me why..

But 'twas in utter peace we spent
Our time with one another,
And I sat there in sweet content,
Communing with my brother.

....

To a Dead Blackbird

Poor blackbird, dead and lying there!
Thy voice no more will charm me,
I'll lift and place thee safely where
No other ill can harm thee.

But, blackbird, there's no need for me
T'indulge in pointless sorrow.
The Death that came today for thee
May come for me tomorrow.

And that poor thing that liest on
The pathway, wet and soddy,
It is not thee, for thou art gone.
It's just an empty body.

Men think heaven's only for mankind,
–They have such selfish natures–
But those who get there soon will find
There's plenty other creatures,

For if Man has a soul in spite
Of all the ill he's done,
Then surely it is only right
That, blackbird, thou hast one.

And when I'm called to my account,
Though I may little merit
Yet there may be a small amount
Just lying to my credit,

Then gratefully I'll soar to where
Thy friends have long been winging,
And happily I'll settle there
To listen to thy singing.

....

The Eagle

Far above, remote and regal,
On his wide majestic wings,
Glides the proud and splendid eagle,
King of birds and bird of kings.

Effortlessly ever riding
On whatever winds may blow,.
Or on still'air presiding
O'er the hills and glens below.

Scanning all his wide dominions
With a monarch's haughty eye,
While his long and pow'rful pinions
Bear him safely in the sky.

In a graceful swoop descending
To inspect some object there,
Then in lazy loops ascending
Into thinner purer air.

Higher still and higher winging
In the cerulean blue,
Higher planes forever bringing
Wider prospects into view.

Wild and free and unmolested,
In his realm of mountains high,
Undisputed, uncontested
Lord and master of the sky.
　　*****************

Bird! 'twould be by necromancy,
Or by some decree divine,
If this poet's feeble fancy
E'er indulged in flights like thine!

Sparrows

Little sparrows on a path,
Close by one another,
Each, with black unwinking eyes,
Searching anxiously the skies,
Making hungry plaintive cries
For their absent mother.

Little mother, small as they,
Busy as a beaver,
Busy hunting all the day
So her cheeping babies may
Soon grow up and fly away,
Fly away and leave her.

Little sparrows, mouths agape,
Feeling mighty hollow,
While she searches far and wide
All the nearby countryside,
Where the juicy morsels hide
That are good to swallow.

Soon she flies back with some worms,
—How a sparrow loves them—
Little need for them to squeak
For she sees each begging beak
Open for the food they seek.
In their mouths she shoves them.

Weary mother; famished brood!
Do they ever thank her?
Never can she take a rest
From her never-ending quest,
And the duties of the nest,
While for food they hanker.

Little mother, grudge them not.
Grudge your children never,
For *your* little mother, too,
Had to work as hard as you,
As all mothers have to do,
And must do for ever.

....

Obsession

I wander down valleys, by tall distant mountains,
Where rivulets run on their way to the sea,
By streamlets and rivers and clear crystal fountains,
But think of the lady who's thinking of me.

I roam by green pastures where cattle are grazing,
In sunshine, perhaps, or the shade of a tree,
By fields where the lambs and their mothers are lazing,
But think of the lady who's thinking of me.

I stray down a street in a town or a city,
Amazed by the crowds and the traffic I see,
Regarding the people with fondness or pity,
But think of the lady who's thinking of me.

Wherever I stray, or I roam, or I wander,
Through cities, or valleys, by fields or the sea,
I gaze all around me with pleasure and wonder,
But think of the lady who's thinking of me.

....

Address to a White Hair

Thou'rt dead so soon in spite of all my care!
I had not looked to find thee on my sleeve
So lifeless and forlorn. Alas! Poor hair!
And yet it is but for myself I grieve,
Since only I can count the labour lost
In rearing thee, which no one can requite,
And I alone, who grew thee, know the cost
Of changing thee from brown to silver-white.
Full many were the troubled, anxious years
I spent on thee, who art of sorrow bred,
And many were the angry, bitter tears
That poured unceasingly about my head.
But stay! Why should I of thy death complain
While hundreds of thy comrades yet remain?

....

Man in Space

This weak and puny creature of the dust;
This little lordling scarce five minutes old,
Dared God and God became. With spirits bold
He braved the very depths of space and thrust
His eager, questing way among the stars
That coldly flared, eternities away,
Aloofly and forlorn. He did not stay,
But onwards pressed and swept away the bars
Twixt Life and Matter, and he saw what was,
And knew what is and what is yet to be.
In awe-struck wonder; shocked; incredulous,
He humble grew and could not bear to see
Such fearsome, awesome majesty. His brain
And senses reeled and he was dust again.

....

The Vision

Dressed in coat of glist'ning black,
Glist'ning with the sea,
Ne'er a word to me he spak,
Ne'er a word to me.

Pale his cheek and dank his hair,
He sighed mournfully,
Looked at me in deep despair,
Looked so woefully.

Loud the wind from o'er the Forth,
Gusting furiously,
Screamed and howled from out the north,
Blowing grievously.

'gainst the bar, the ocean wild
Raged right angrily,
As to me he sadly smiled,
Smiled unhappily.

Blending with the blinding rain,
Pouring endlessly,
Far from me he went again,
Went so soundlessly.

Swift the tears came tae my een,
Came so violently,
When they brought him home yestre'en,
Brought his silently.

Dressed in coat of glist'ning black,
Glist'ning with the sea,
Ne'er a word to me he spak,
Ne'er a word to me.
....

The Scottish Express

The doors are slammed, the whistle shrills,
The platform crowd is waved away,
The din of noisy laughter stills,
The platform starts to glide and sway
And as it steadily retreats
The passengers resume their seats
And with relief they settle back
As o'er the points along the track
The train proceeds and gathers speed
As factories and homes recede
The farther we go the faster we travel
With hardly a jolt and scarcely a rattle
We hasten by farms and villages too
And scarce know the towns we are hurrying through
For signs at the stations are flickering past
We're travelling now so incredibly fast
As though the devil was close on our heels
And so increasing the speed of our wheels
Through Wolverhampton and Stafford to Crewe
—We only stop for a minute or two—
Then hurrying onwards and soon we find
That Preston and Lancaster are behind
Now faster and faster and faster we press
For nothing must hinder the Scottish Express
As it eats up the railway lines mile after mile
And pauses but briefly when reaching Carlisle
Then checking our tickets to see they're in order
We pass over Sark – and are over the Border.

Jean

When I got on the bus for Perth,
A winsome woman caught my e'en.
I saw the fairest face on Earth –
The face of the engaging Jean.

She looked up at me with a smile,
The like of which I'd never seen,
And longing filled me to beguile
The heart from out th'endearing Jean.

I was enraptured by her voice,
As friendly glances passed between
Us, and I could not but rejoice
That I had met th'entrancing Jean.

Attachment soon between us grew,
As we ignored the passing scene,
And when she said 'farewell' I knew
I'd ne'er forget th'enchanting Jean.

Of course I've been in love before,
Indeed in love I've often been,
But ne'er as much as I adore
The dear, delightful, charming Jean.

On Seeing a Statue of an Aged Couple: Oslo 1977

In a block of stone he found them,
Withered, wrinkled, aged, done,
Hidden in the granite round them,
Patiently awaiting one
Who, with vision deep inside him
And his genius to guide him,
Trod the pathway to the stone
That was known to him alone.

With his chisel, chipping gently,
Chipping with the greatest care,
Cautiously and reverently
Seeking those he *knew* were there,
Never tiring, never ceasing
From his task of soon releasing
From their prison, cold and grim,
Those he knew awaited him.

When at last they were discovered
Seated there in solitude,
Lovingly they were uncovered
In their touching attitude.
Skilfully he then unwrapped them
From the granite that entrapped them,
Till, at length, came into view
Something greater than he knew.

Two old friends, their ending sharing,
Silent, still, their journey done,
Each, while waiting, only caring,
Caring for the other one.
Still they sit, remote, unheeding,
Lost in thoughts of days receding
Into time and empty air,
Careless of the people there.

On a slope above the city,
By a column white and tall,
Sits this gem of love and pity,
Waiting to reproach us all,
Telling us that present sorrow
May seem distant joy tomorrow;
That the comfort love can lend
Gives us courage at the end.

....

Sculptor   Gustav Vigeland
****

A Poet's Prayer

Oh, Lord, hear Thou the humble prayer
Of one who would thy servant be,
Make him no more his burden bear
That he may better honour Thee.

In awe before Thy works I stand
And see perfection ev'rywhere,
The craftsmanship and loving care
That are alone at Thy command.

I would that I could spend my days
In writng verse and singing praise
About Thy wonders, so that men
Might turn to simple things again.

But, Lord, thou gav'st me eyes to see;
A mind that can appreciate
The beauty of simplicity,
Yet made'st me inarticulate.

So in humility I come,
—Who must obey in ev'rything—
Thou gavest me the urge to sing,
Why, then, should'st Thou have made me dumb?

Emotions locked within my breast
Forever seek to be expressed,
Tumultuous thoughts churn in my mind,
Yet they can no expression find.

Lord, grant to me my soul's desire,
That I may reach the minds of men,
I *must* a silver tongue acquire,
I beg one of thee, Lord, Amen.

The Woman

She took me to her room. We were
Like old friends as I talked to her
Of griefs that had o'ertaken me
And friends who had forsaken me.
I said I could not carry on,
But after I had dwelt upon
My troubles for a long, long while,
She smiled a sympathetic smile
And gave to me, in words sincere,
The comfort that I longed to hear.
She gave me hope and courage, too,
And only for a pound or two.

She took me in her little bed
And put her arms around my head,
Then drew it down upon her breast
And there I found the peace and rest
Which I had so long been denied,
While she all night a love contrived.
She kissed me o'er and o'er again,
As in her arms I lay, and then
Beneath the blinds the sunlight shone,
And so I knew the night was gone.
But so was grief and sorrow too,
And only for a pound or two.

....

The Deid Punter

Auld Tam MacPhail at last has gane!
Where'er he be, pair sinner,
May's fav'rites start at ten tae ane
An' ev'ry yin a winner.

For doon on Earth he always lost,
An' wis by luck neglected.
E'en when his horses cam' in first
They'd be by judge rejected.

But money wis tae sic a wan
Made anely tae be riskit.
He'd tak his losses like a man,
---Frae his wife's shoppin' basket.

Nae wunner bookies smiled tae see
Auld Tam MacPhail acomin'!
'twis he wha kept them happily
In whusky an' in wummen.

I ne'er heard tell o' bookie win
A place amang the holy.
Sic a thing wad be a sin
An' sair afront the godly.

Sae who's oor Tam tae hae a bet,
Wi'oot a bookie there,
On wha cams in through heaven's yett
An' wha gangs itherwhere?

But wait! Ah Tam ye hiv it made,
-If ye be no in hell, man,
If bets by angels are na laid,
Then mak a buik yirsel', man.

....

The Motorway

The motorway's an eerie road
To drive upon at night.
The motorway's a dreary road
Twixt dusk and morning light.

I feel I scarcely need to drive,
The van and I are one,
As though, indeed, it were alive,
Or rails it moved upon.

Between the broken lines we pass,
While bright the cats' eyes gleam.
Advancing headlights dim and flash,
Though few and far between.

And in the dark, on either hand,
Long necklaces of light
Keep vigil o'er the sleeping land,
In blue or brilliant white.

Now Helen must be sleeping sound.
I see her huddled form,
A motionless, untidy mound,
All cuddled up and warm.

I wonder if she got that hat
That she was on about.
I'll get that new thick overcoat
Unless my luck is out.

I'm glad I bought her those few tights,
Just for a small surprise.
"Why don't you dim your bloody lights?
They're blazing in my eyes!"

It looks as though there's been a crash,
The cops are ev'rywhere,
They stand around and blue lights flash.
An ambulance is there.

Oh! There it is! It's been head-on
By looks of it. My God!
The car's a wreck and upside down!
He must be dead, poor sod.

I'm getting sleepy now, I must
Be careful How I go.
I wonder if Red Rum came first.
Just fifteen miles to go.

It's getting light now. There's the sun,
Now ends another trip.
For some a new day's work's begun,
For me some tea, then kip.

....

Advice on the Training of Children

The members of this savage clan
Have driven many an honest man
To drink or hari kari.
And so I tender my advice,
Painstaking, thoughtful and precise,
To those about to marry.

You ought to give them ev'ry care
And cherish them, no matter where
Their devilry may lead them,
But it is sure the little brutes
Will turn from their bizarre pursuits
And bite the hands which feed them.

You may, of course, give way to rage
And leave them in an orphanage,
Then cheerfully forget them,
A course which will commend itself
To any dad left to himself,
But many wives won't let them.

Some parents, more naive than some,
Think blackmail them will overcome,
But they must be demented,
For surely they must realise
That children in it specialise
And 'twas by them invented.

Be careful of the means you use,
And certainly don't cause a bruise
When children you're chastising.
A sandbag should be used instead
Of knuckle-dusters, lengths of lead
Or bits of iron piping.

If you, perhaps, some lectures give
To teach them that *you too* must live,
I doubt if they'll imbibe them.
I recommend you use a ruse,
So use a ruse I used to use
And with a story bribe them.

....

To Baby Martin

Welcome, little stranger, lying
Peacefully upon your bed,
It is time to look around you
At the years which lie ahead.

Open up those heavy eyelids,
Turn your head and look above,
See the happy faces gazing
Down at you with eyes of love.

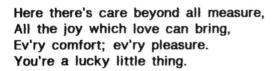

Here there's care beyond all measure,
All the joy which love can bring,
Ev'ry comfort; ev'ry pleasure.
You're a lucky little thing.

May your life be long and happy,
Joys be many, troubles few,
Loving some and loved by many,
BUT it's largely up to you.

....
30.3.1991

63

A Man's Complaint

You mighty gods of long ago,
–Egyptian, Greek and Roman–
There's something I would like to know
And it is "Why had you to go
And rashly make a woman?"

The thought itself was rather good,
–Between you all you hatched it–
Amusing too, though faintly crude,
It's perils, though, not understood
And so you went and botched it.

I sometimes thought that often she
Said more than she intended,
–Her words were poured out endlessly!–
Shame of it is she could not see
That least said soonest mended.

And sometimes when I wrote to her
–In either prose or sonnet–
A letter, just to pleasure her,
She'd put –one could depend on her–
The worst construction on it.

But where the fault is I can't say,
–No time to linger on it–
However, be whate'er it may,
I hope that you yourselves one day
Will lay a finger on it.

The failure of your kindly plan
Is much to be lamented,
–The flaw's been there since time began–
Repair your blunder, if you can,
And I'll be well contented.

....

The Question

No doubt when it is time to die,
–I must die soon or late–
My simple soul will upwards fly
And knock at Heaven's gate.

And, after I have knocked a while,
Saint Peter will appear
And greet me with a wintry smile,
Impassive and austere.

And then he'll ask me who I am,
–As if he didn't know it–
And I shall say "Why, I am Sam.
You must know me – the poet!"

He'll tell me, much to my surprise,
"You can't come here to dwell.
You're much too bad for Paradise,
– Though much too good for Hell."

"You'd best return at once to Earth:
Continue writing verse
And come back when you're better
Or considerably worse."

So I'll return, deferring to
His sainthood, but sometimes
I'll think "Was he referring to
My morals or my rhymes?"

Ambition

What do I want?
             A quiet mind
And all my dear ones nigh me,
A piece of land to call my own
And happy mem'ries by me.

When Death comes by with friendly smile
And lingers close beside me,
And, to encourage me the while,
Holds out his hand to guide me
What shall I want?
             A quiet mind
And all my dear ones nigh me,
A piece of land for me alone
And happy mem'ries by me.

....

Vale

Leaves have their time to fall,
Flowers to wilther,
Wild winds will blow them all
Hither and thither.

On the cold earth they'll die,
Faded, rain—battered,
And their small corses lie
Where they were scattered.

Leaves have their time to fall.
All whom we cherish,
Must answer Death's mute call,
All of us perish.

....

The Editor,
The Scots Independent,
Stirling.

Dear Sir,

About thirty years ago, in the fond belief that I would live long enough to enjoy life in an independent Scotland, I wrote my own epitaph.

At my present age of eighty, it may be that I shall not live quite long enough to enjoy Independence Day and, therefore, my words would be inappropriate on my gravestone. However, if any other independence supporter cares to use it a few years hence, he or she is most welcome to do so.

Yours for Scotland
Sam MacEachan.

Epitaph

My friends, thy sighs and tears restrain,
Pray, do not weep so mournfully!
Thy sighs and tears are all in vain.
There is no need to mourn for me,
For I, who have from Earth been torn
To lie below within this plot,
Unwittingly a Briton born
Was very pleased to die a Scot.

....

IN HONOUR

The following letter and poem are published in order to honour the memory of Donald F. MacLean, born Glasgow 1880, who sent them to my parents in celebration of my birth, it having taken place on the 14th February, 1910.

With sadness, one remembers that he was killed in battle during the world war of 1914–1918.

. . . .

Glasgow
February, 1910.

To Mr and Mrs MacEachan.

Enclosed you will find a few lines of poetry
composed to celebrate the birth of your little
son. They perhaps do not contain the sentiment
that is required to do justice to the subject,
but they do possess sentiment that is sincere.
Their claim to originality can not be doubted
and if you can find any pleasure in accepting
these lines I shall feel well paid for the labour,
which was indeed a pleasure to me. If, however,
there is anything that you find not harmonious,
I will be pleased to try to eliminate anything
that might seem offensive. I again ask you to
accept them with all the best wishes which I
have for your little son whose coming inspired
the poem.

I hope that you are well and enjoying, as I am,
the best of health.

Yours in friendship

Donald F. MacLean

Lines to Baby

1st   Welcome, Little Stranger, welcome
Welcome to this vale of tears,
To this land of strife and turmoil,
Sorrow, anguish, care and fears.

2nd   'tis with joy they hail thine advent,
Two fond hearts who love thee so,
For it's happiness and pleasure
They alone can fully know.

3rd   They indeed were very lonely
Till thou came'st their hearts to cheer,
Chasing all the gloom around them
With thy radiant smile so clear.

4th   In the garden, 'midst the bushes,
Birds their sweetest songs may sing,
But thy cries are sweeter music
With their buoyant, joyous ring.

5th   Orbs that glisten in the heavens
Light the skies with splendour bright,
But thine eyes to them seem brighter,
Sparkling in the morning light.

6th   Scenes of grandeur rise before me,
But are of their beauty shorn
When compared to parents standing,.
Contemplating their first-born.

7th   There is naught in life's great sequel
By the hand of mortal made,
That in purity can equal
Love's untarnished hallowed babe.

8th   Thou art Nature's contribution
And all earthly scenes so grand
Pale before thy wond'rous beauty,
Fashioned by the Master Hand.

9th   Winning love from all around thee,
Lighting up with radiance clear,
Mother's face, serene and loving,
Father's, tender, kind and dear.

10th   May'st thou grow their love to cherish
And when they're beneath the sod,
Follow still their path of virtue,
Onwards, upwards to thy God.